Spiritual DISEASES

of the

Unbridled

Tongue

M.J. Welcome

Other Books by M. J. Welcome:

Overcome Secret Sins in 15 Days

Battling for the Light

The 21-Day Crucifixion Challenge

SMART PUBLISHING HOUSE
A Division of MDW Consulting Group
Far Rockaway, New York
www.smartpublishinghouse.com

Editing | Layout S.M.A.R.T Copy Designs
Proofreaders | Mary Ball | Matteel Welcome | JS Fer
S.M.A.R.T Copy Designs
www.smartcopydesignsinc.com

First Published by Smart Publishing House 07/12/16

Library of Congress Control Number: 2016911600

ISBN-13: 978-0982540091
ISBN-10: 0982540094

Note: This publication is intended to provide helpful information on the subject matter covered. It is sold with the understanding that the author and publisher are not rendering professional services in the book. If the reader requires personal or spiritual advice, a competent professional should be consulted.

All Scripture, unless otherwise stated, is taken from the King James Version of the Holy Bible. Hebrew and Greek meanings from Strong's Concordance.

Printed in the U.S.A.

SMART
PUBLISHING HOUSE
...the smart place to publish

TABLE OF CONTENTS

ACKNOWLEDGEMENTS

*"Worthy is the Lamb who was
slain, to receive power, and
riches, and wisdom, and
strength, and honour, and glory,
and blessing."*
—Revelation 5:12

J esus deserves all the praise for all that is accomplished in this book. His example, words of counsel, the open door that he unlocked for believers to have access to God the Father, and for outlining our clear purpose as sons of God.

To Holy Spirit who led and gave direction throughout this process, making things clearer and answering my many questions with timely unction's and sound scriptural doctrine.

To God the Father, Your love is incomprehensible and unfathomable. I am so grateful that you love me and have made a way for me to love myself as I walk in the steps of Christ Jesus. Thank you!

To my husband and children, thank you for your support and encouragement as I worked on this devotional. Words cannot express my appreciation and love for you all.

John, as always your insights and questions were invaluable. May the Lord continue to bless you as you write, critique, and edit to advance the Kingdom of God!

INTRODUCTION

Greetings in the name of Jehovah, the Existing One!

The tongue is the smallest member of the human body, yet it can be boastful, a fire starter, full of deadly poison, unruly, evil, and unpredictable. It can speak forth-blessing one minute and curses the next. It stirs up strife, division and confusion, but can also release words of peace, gentleness wisdom, and love.

As believers, our tongues are to release good fruit at all times. Impartial, peaceful, and hypocrisy free fruit. Our tongues are to discharge life into the earth, our relationships, and in every situation.

This is a tall order, for the tongue is **unbridled**. Who can tame it? Who can put it under subjection? We can through the power of God in Christ Jesus.

> *"We can do all thing through Jesus who strengthens us."*
> —Philippians 4:13

In this book, we will identify different types of tongues and the dangers they pose. We will also learn how to subdue our *unbridled tongues* God's way so we can be victorious in Christ Jesus.

Learning how to release life with our words is a process, but with dedication and perseverance, we will overcome reclaiming our tongues for the Lord.

Here's to bridling *your* TONGUE!

M.J. Welcome

DAY 1

Disease of

CORRUPT COMMUNICATION

*"Let no corrupt communication
proceed out of your mouth, but
that which is good to the use of
edifying, that it may minister
grace unto the hearers."*
— Ephesians 4:29

Paul's declaration in Ephesians 4:29 communicates more than we might imagine. The Greek word ***sapros*** (G4550) is used for both the word ***let*** and ***corrupt*** in the above verse. ***Sapros*** means to become unfit for use, become worn out, be of poor quality, to be putrid, and rotten. The root word used is ***sepo*** (G4595) means to make corrupt, to destroy, or to become corrupted.

When we plug the Greek meanings into the verse, we get a vivid picture of what Paul instructs believers to refrain from doing. Let no rotten, putrefied, bad, or worthless speech flow forth from your mouth. For it corrupts, destroys, and will cause *you* to become of poor quality and unfit for use.

The speaker has power to bring about life or death. If he chooses to engage in corrupt communication then death will occur and the glorious purpose God had in mind for him would be derailed and eventually destroyed.

If he listens to Paul's counsel; then he will be fit for use in the kingdom work of the Lord.

> *"Death and life are in the power of the tongue: and they that love it shall eat the fruit thereof."*
> —Proverbs 18:21

The words that flow from our mouths should produce fruit, not just for others to be influenced by either for good or evil, but so that we may eat the fruit and reap the rewards thereof.

DAY 1

As believers, we signed up to allow God to recreate us. Our old selves are to die so that a new version of us in the image of Christ can manifest. This transformation is the sanctifying work of God, but in order for it to be realized; we must continually consent and agree to His process.

"Knowing this, that our old man is crucified with him, that the body of sin might be destroyed, that henceforth we should not serve sin."
—Romans 6:6

"Jesus answered and said unto him, Verily, verily, I say unto thee, Except a man be born again, he cannot see the kingdom of God."
—John 3:3

God always gives us a choice (Joshua 24:15). He allows us to register our vote. Every conversation we engage in either throws a ballet for the Lord to continue His work or it opens the way for the enemy to usurp what belongs to God.

"In meekness instructing those that oppose themselves; if God peradventure will give them repentance to the acknowledging of the truth; and that they may recover themselves out of the snare of the devil, who are taken captive by him at his will."
—2 Timothy 2:25-26

What is your choice today?

Prayer

Heavenly Father, please forgive me where I have engaged in corrupt communication. Enable me to place my conversations under the Lordship of Jesus Christ. I know that I can do all things thorough Jesus, amen.

"I can do all things through Christ which strengtheneth me."
Philippians 4:13

Activity

As you go throughout the day, be conscious about the conversations you have with yourself and with others. Does it glorify God? Will it bear fruit for the kingdom? Is it honoring to Christ Jesus?

Those things that are edifying continue to do them. If they are not, you should judge them and seek God's help for their removal.

> *"But he that is spiritual judgeth all things, yet he himself is judged of no man."*
> —1 Corinthians 2:15

> *"Ask, and it shall be given you; seek, and ye shall find; knock, and it shall be opened unto you: For every one that asketh receiveth; and he that seeketh findeth; and to him that knocketh it shall be opened."*
> —Matthew 7:7-8

Disease of the

BELITTLING TONGUE

"He that is void of wisdom despiseth his neighbour: but a man of understanding holdeth his peace."
—Proverbs 11:12

The Hebrew word for **despiseth** is **buwz** which means to hold in contempt or as insignificant.

The American Heritage College Dictionary defines **belittling** as to represent, or speak of as contemptibly small or unimportant, to disparage, and to cause to seem less than another. This qualifies as corrupt communication for it does not edify or build up another.

"Let your speech be alway with grace, seasoned with salt, that ye may know how ye ought to answer every man."
—Colossians 4:6

*"Let no corrupt communication
proceed out of your mouth, but
that which is good to the use of
edifying, that it may minister
grace unto the hearers."*
—Ephesians 4:29

The word corrupt is defined as tainted,
perverse, depraved, dishonest, spoiled, or
rotten; thus, when our communication is
corrupt it is neither wholesome, healthy,
nor full of virtue.

The Bible tells us that life and death is in
the tongue (Proverbs 18:21). When we
speak to people, we are to supply life with
our words not death. Do your words build
up or tear down? Do you denigrate or
disparage with your remarks? Or do you
edify or encourage?

In 1 Thessalonians, we are given sound
counsel.

*"Wherefore comfort yourselves
together, and edify one another,
even as also ye do."*
—1 Thessalonians 5:11

We are to edify, build up, and comfort one another. Our communication should be life giving; if it is not, then it is **corrupt**. If it tears down another, it belittles them and treats them as if they are insignificant.

Next time, when you are tempted to find fault with how an employee is working, choose instead to praise and encourage him to do better. When your child fails to do something right, you should coach him or her by pointing out ways he or she can make better choices.

If correction is needed, do it the way Christ would, in truth without tearing down, belittling, or condemning another. Help to build others as God does with honest and sincere words.

Unify as Christ did on the cross. He made a way for us to know the Father intimately. And as our advocate in heaven he continually speaks words that will enable us to become more like him with the guidance of Holy Spirit which will lead us to *all truth* (John 16:13 and Revelation 2-3).

DAY 2

Our thoughts dictate what flows from our mouths. If we think negatively, our words will reflect that negativity, eventually. Our only safeguard is to have our minds renewed.

"And be not conformed to this world: but be ye transformed by the renewing of your mind, that ye may prove what is that good, and acceptable, and perfect, will of God."
—Romans 12:2

"And be renewed in the spirit of your mind; And that ye put on the new man, which after God is created in righteousness and true holiness."
—Ephesians 4:23-24

Be willing to subdue the old nature through self-discipline, self-control, and self-denial.

*"Mortify therefore your members
which are upon the earth;
fornication, uncleanness,
inordinate affection, evil
concupiscence, and covetousness,
which is idolatry: For which
things' sake the wrath of God
cometh on the children of
disobedience: In the which ye
also walked some time, when ye
lived in them."*
—Colossians 3:5-7

Jesus sent help through Holy Spirit. He will abide with believers forever.

*"And I will pray the Father, and
he shall give you another
Comforter, that he may abide
with you for ever;"*
—John 14:16

It is through the equipping of Holy Spirit that we can exercise self-control (temperance) over our tongues.

*"But the fruit of the Spirit is love,
joy, peace, longsuffering,
gentleness, goodness, faith,
Meekness, temperance: against
such there is no law."*
—Galatians 5:22-23

As we continue to live spiritually in Christ Jesus, the fruits of the spirit will manifest in us, in our lives, and through our conversations.

Prayer

Oh Lord, I bless you for making a way for me to glorify you as I live and speak on the earth. I thank you for sending Your Spirit to dwell with me forever. Father, forgive me of every sinful thought and word. I desire to have the fruits of Your Spirit manifest in my life. Support me, I pray, amen.

> *"For the eyes of the LORD run to and fro throughout the whole earth, to shew himself strong in the behalf of them whose heart is perfect toward him. Herein thou hast done foolishly: therefore from henceforth thou shalt have wars."*
> —2 Chronicles 16:9

Activity

God's process is a life journey, just as it takes time for a seed to grow into a tree and produce fruit so it is with our transformation into the likeness of Christ Jesus.

Patience is the key. God is longsuffering; He is enduring and full of compassion toward the children of men.

"Among whom also we all had our conversation in times past in the lusts of our flesh, fulfilling the desires of the flesh and of the mind; and were by nature the children of wrath, even as others. But God, who is rich in mercy, for his great love wherewith he loved us, Even when we were dead in sins, hath quickened us together with Christ, (by grace ye are saved;)"
—Ephesians 2:3-5

We were dead in our sins, but He brought us to life in Christ Jesus. Let us glorify Him with spiritually bridled tongues rather than natural tongues.

Today let us give the gift of patience to those we encounter. Let us bridle our tongue by refraining from belittling thoughts and words.

Disease of the

CYNICAL TONGUE

"The people thus contended with Moses and spoke, saying, "If only we had perished when our brothers perished before the LORD!"
—Numbers 20:3

What does it mean to have a cynical tongue? Cynical, is to believe that people are motivated by selfish or callous calculating motives. It is the expression of jaded, scornful skepticism or negativity. But what does this sound like?

On the job, have you ever come across an individual who always has a negative word for every season? People could be laughing or having fun, but this person always has a complaint or a scornful word to say about the company, the boss, or a coworker. When that individual comes into the room the atmosphere changes, it is like the life, energy, and even light is sucked out of the air. When the person starts to speak, it is as if poison had been released. The atmosphere changed— it became heavy, lifeless, toxic, and dead.

The cynical tongues of the Children of Israel and those of his family assaulted Moses according to Numbers 12:7-11. The spirit of negativity contaminated and poisoned all those who heard the words.

> *"And Miriam and Aaron spake against Moses because of the Ethiopian woman whom he had married: for he had married an Ethiopian woman. And they said, Hath the Lord indeed spoken only by Moses? hath he not spoken also by us? And the Lord heard it."*
> —Numbers 12:1-2

Let us not deceive ourselves, cynical speech is offensive to God and He will address it, and it will not be a pleasant experience! Mariam experienced God's correction first hand and it was not a feel good moment (Hebrews 12:6 and Proverbs 3:12).

"And the anger of the Lord was kindled against them; and he departed. And the cloud departed from off the tabernacle; and, behold, Miriam became leprous, white as snow: and Aaron looked upon Miriam, and, behold, she was leprous."
—Numbers 12:9-10

DAY 3

*"Unto the pure all things are
pure: but unto them that are
defiled and unbelieving is
nothing pure; but even their
mind and conscience is defiled.
They profess that they know
God; but in works they deny him,
being abominable, and
disobedient, and unto every good
work reprobate."*
—Titus 1:15-16

D o we know God? Do our thoughts, words, and actions testify that we are intimately acquainted with God?

Are we distrustful without cause? Do we speak negatively about others? Are our conclusions or observations discerned through the Spirit of God or from the corruption of our natural hearts, and minds?

In John 8:44, Jesus spoke words that seem negative and to some may have come across cynical. However, every word he spoke was spirit led. They were true words, not malicious attacks motivated from the flesh (Matthew 23:23-34).

John the Baptist also spoke harsh words to the crowds that listened to him (Luke 3:7). The difference between cynical words and his words was that John's words were based in truth. Jesus and John used true words to expose lurking darkness.

Mariam's words were birthed from the flesh. She wielded them as a weapon designed for a destructive purpose. Let us take counsel with the Lord in order to discern truth, before we speak.

Prayer

Heavenly Father, I have not used my mouth as an instrument of righteousness. I have spoken things that were negative and cynical. Lord, heal my tongue and forgive my sin. Let me speak what is right and pleasing in your sight, amen.

> *"But he was wounded for our transgressions, he was bruised for our iniquities: the chastisement of our peace was upon him; and with his stripes we are healed."*
> —Isaiah 53:5

Activity

Take time today to reflect on your recent conversations. Sift through them and identify words or thoughts where you were cynical (negative). If you spoke those words to others, you should go and make it right with the help of the Lord.

> *"Death and life are in the power of the tongue: and they that love it shall eat the fruit thereof."*
> —Proverbs 18:21

Your mission is to produce and encourage life!

Disease of the

GRIEVOUS TONGUE

"A soft answer turneth away wrath: but grievous words stir up anger."
—Proverbs 15:1

If you look up synonyms for the word grievous you may find words like terrible, grave, dire, severe, or harsh which can be used to replace it. Proverbs 15:1 tells us that grievous words stir up anger while a soft answer turns anger away.

Why do grievous words cause anger? Could it be because it causes an offense? Or that it hurts feelings? Or because it belittles?

I remember giving my eldest son advice about his schoolwork in a sharp tone using harsh words. I was upset, tired, and annoyed so I did not activate the brakes on my mouth. My son got angry because I provoked him to anger.

> *"And, ye fathers, provoke not*
> *your children to wrath: but bring*
> *them up in the nurture and*
> *admonition of the Lord."*
> —Ephesians 6:4

> *"Fathers, provoke not your*
> *children to anger, lest they be*
> *discouraged."*
> —Colossians 3:21

Later, I repented and asked for his forgiveness. My son did not find fault with the counsel, but rather the delivery.

Our words, according to Proverbs 15:4 are to be a spring of life. If our words cause wounds or provoke anger, how can life spring from it?

If you find yourself speaking grievous, critical, dreadful, awful, or crushing words ask God to salt your tongue with His grace and love.

> *"But speaking the truth in love,*
> *let us grow in every way into*
> *Him who is the head--Christ."*
> —Ephesians 4:15

Allow God to transform your mouth into a spring of life that honors Him. Today is a good day to start, and with practice, your words will be a blessing to all who hear them!

DAY 4

The fallen nature of man is fault finding, critical, and at times crushing. Our words can cause deep wounds to ourselves and to others.

We are called to love our neighbors as we do ourselves (Mark 12:31). What happens if we do not love ourselves? How then can we love others?

True love can only be taught by the one who is love (1 John 4:8). Each of us must learn God's way of loving. His love is freeing, uplifting, correcting, edifying, and true. It is a longsuffering and persevering love.

Let us give to others what we have freely received from God through Christ Jesus, words of truth that build us up and does not crush us.

"The spirit of a man will sustain his infirmity; but a wounded spirit who can bear?"
—Proverbs 18:14

"The LORD is nigh unto them that are of a broken heart; and saveth such as be of a contrite spirit."
—Psalms 34:18

*"A merry heart doeth good like a
medicine: but a broken spirit
drieth the bones."*
—Proverbs 17:22

Prayer

Lord, help me to have a wholesome tongue. One that is anointed with truth and love. One that is uplifting and merciful. It is my earnest desire to please you in my conversations. Help me to release words that deliver and heal. Where I have crushed others please forgive me and release healing for them in the name of Jesus, name.

*"A wholesome tongue is a tree of
life: but perverseness therein is a
breach in the spirit."*
—Proverbs 15:4

Activity

As you go throughout the day, search out opportunities where you can release a word of truth or healing. Ask Holy Spirit to guide you in this endeavor.

*"For as many as are led by the Spirit
of God, they are the sons of God."*
—Romans 8:14

Remember that you are a son of God in the making, and creation is waiting with great anticipation for you!

"For the earnest expectation of the creature waiteth for the manifestation of the sons of God."
—Romans 8:19

Disease of the

SCORNFUL TONGUE

*"Blessed is the man that walketh
not in the counsel of the ungodly,
nor standeth in the way of
sinners, nor sitteth in the seat of
the scornful."*
—Psalms 1:1

Boasters, mockers, and the arrogant are those who possess a scornful tongue! The Hebrew word **luwts** provides the root understanding for the word scornful.

This type of person encapsulates what God does not delight in (Jeremiah 9:23-24). A spiritual (righteous) man should avoid such company.

A blessed person will not walk with the ungodly, stand with sinners, or sit with the scornful.

If we are boastful or arrogant, let us make up our mind **today** that we will be the blessed person David describes Psalms 1:1.

If we associate with scornful people, let us divorce ourselves from them. Let us from this day onward follow the path of the righteous. Let us do as David has counseled in Psalms 15:4, which is to despise those who practice sin but love and honor those who bless the Lord.

> *"Boast not thyself of to morrow; for thou knowest not what a day may bring forth. Let another man praise thee, and not thine own mouth; a stranger, and not thine own lips."*
> —Proverbs 27:1-2

> *"That, according as it is written, He that glorieth, let him glory in the Lord."*
> —1 Corinthians 1:31

Our objective as children of God is to do what pleases Him and to engage in what brings our Father delight.

"Thus saith the Lord, Let not the wise man glory in his wisdom, neither let the mighty man glory in his might, let not the rich man glory in his riches: But let him that glorieth glory in this, that he understandeth and knoweth me, that I am the Lord which exercise lovingkindness, judgment, and righteousness, in the earth: for in these things I delight, saith the Lord."
—Jeremiah 9:23-24

DAY 5

If you've ever played or watch sports then you are familiar with boasting. Muhammad Ali was made famous in part, for his boasting in and out of the ring. Unfortunately, his boasts have caught up to him.

Boasting comes at a cost. God lends us time, energy, and opportunity. We have nothing of our own even though the Lord allows us to use these gifts as we see fit.

The foolish man believes that he possess talents, wisdom, and strength aside from God. He believes that he deserves the credit for the benefits God has generously bestowed on him (Matthew 5:45 and Romans 11:29). God has equipped man with gifts and talents, which were intended for His purpose and not our own. They are to bring him glory in the earth.

Yet many refuse to accept or acknowledge God for their gifts, talents, riches, wisdom, health, strength or prosperity.

Let this not be our lot in life. Let us boast always in God and His Christ.

Let us boast about His goodness, faithfulness, and His equipping of His children.

Let us refrain from mocking others, for if we do we are walking in our own ungodly lusts after the similitude of the enemy of God (Ezekiel 36).

> *"How that they told you there should be mockers in the last time, who should walk after their own ungodly lusts."*
> —Jude 1:18

We are not to wear the shame of the enemy. When we engage in this type of communication, we are acting like heathens who have no relationship with God. It is the Father's desire that His children refrain from wearing the filthy garments of the enemy.

Jesus paid the price for us to have righteous garments. It is time for the enemy to wear his own shame.

*"Prophesy therefore concerning
the land of Israel, and say unto
the mountains, and to the hills, to
the rivers, and to the valleys,
Thus saith the Lord God; Behold,
I have spoken in my jealousy and
in my fury, because ye have
borne the shame of the heathen:
Therefore thus saith the Lord
God; I have lifted up mine hand,
Surely the heathen that are about
you, they shall bear their shame."*
—Ezekiel 36:6-7

Prayer

Bless your Holy and Righteous name, oh Lord. I thank you for intervening on my behalf. I thank you for deliverance from the hands of the enemy. For deliverance from scornful communication. Help me to walk in faith believing (2 Corinthians 5:7) that I have the victory in this area (1 Corinthians 15:57). Help me never to doubt you (James 1:6). Lord honor your name in the earth subdue the mocking, arrogant, and boastful spirit and lift up the Spirit of Jesus in me (Philippians 1:19, Romans 8:9, and Romans 8:11) amen.

"Therefore say unto the house of Israel, thus saith the Lord God; I do not this for your sakes, O house of Israel, but for mine holy name's sake, which ye have profaned among the heathen, whither ye went."
—Ezekiel 36:22

Activity

Take time today to give God thanks for all the good things He has done for you. Brag on Him. Lift Him up with a sincere heart.

Praise Him for endowing you with gifts and talents. Bless Him for providing for you. Look around yourself, recognize the uniqueness of others, their talents and gifts and offer thanksgiving unto God on their behalf.

Release the sweet smell of incense before God. It is time to throw down the scornful (boastful) tongue.

DAY 6

Disease of the

FALSE TONGUE

"Thou shalt not bear false witness against thy neighbour."
—Exodus 20:16

What does it mean to bear false witness? According to the Hebrew meaning, the word *false* is deceit, fraud, deception, to lie, trick, cheat, speaking with a false tongue, swearing falsely, and to disappoint. It is when one is false to one's faith or when one breaks a covenant.

The Merriam-Webster online dictionary defines *false* as "not genuine, intentionally untrue, adjusted or made so as to deceive, intended or tending to mislead." Therefore, the core of the false tongue is deception and falsehood.

In the beginning, the Serpent (bore false witness) deceived Eve by speaking with a false tongue (Genesis 3). He was crafty and used trickery against her. The result being she was dishonest and untrue to her faith in God thus she became a covenant breaker.

The Bible tells us that the devil is a liar and the father of lies.

> *"Ye are of your father the devil, and the lusts of your father ye will do. He was a murderer from the beginning, and abode not in the truth, because there is no truth in him. When he speaketh a lie, he speaketh of his own: for he is a liar, and the father of it."*
> —John 8:44

When we use the devil's crafty tools to deceive or deal falsely with others we are operating as one of his children.

The Word of God is clear we are not to deal in falsehood. We are not to cheat, trick, or deal falsely with our neighbors. God bans fraudulence in any form.

We are called to speak the truth, the simple, unadulterated truth so help us God.

> *"But speaking the truth in love, may grow up into him in all things, which is the head, even Christ:"*
> —Ephesians 4:15

<u>DAY 6</u>

Falsehood is dangerous for it knows no bounds and it can cost a life or rob others of their freedom.

As believers, we are called to be truthful in all that we do. We are to uphold the standard of God. There is no way that we can uphold or exhibit the righteousness of God with false tongues.

There is no falsehood in God, he does not lie, it is against his nature (Numbers 23:19). As his sons, we are called to be the same.

If we choose to love truth, we will eat the fruit of truth. If however, we love falsehood we will eat the bitter and rotten fruit thereof.

"Death and life are in the power of the tongue: and they that love it shall eat the fruit thereof."
—Proverbs 18:21

Prayer

Father, I thank you for your correction of love. I ask that you convict me where in I have falsely spoken against my neighbor. I ask that you would forgive my sin and help me to make it right. Lord help me to speak the truth in love *always*. Help me to be a true witness, in all that I do and say, in Jesus name, amen.

Activity

With the leading of Holy Spirit think over your recent statements. Were they true? Was there any deceit, trickery, or lies intermingled with your words? If so, seek Holy Spirits guidance on how to make it right with your neighbor.

Remember you can do all things through Jesus Christ who strengthens you (Philippians 4:13)!

Disease of the

TACTLESS TONGUE

Let your speech be alway with grace, seasoned with salt, that ye may know how ye ought to answer every man.
—Colossians 4:6

The tactless tongue is marred with hast and insensitivity. A tongue that speaks before the adequate processing of thoughts. Once its words are released, human carnage is left in its wake, yet the tactless tongue may be oblivious to this fact.

In some cases, it may be aware of it, but it justifies itself with sayings such as, "Just being real," or "I have to tell it like it is," or "It's who I am."

Colossians 4:6, commands believers to speak always with grace and to season their words with salt so they will know how to answer every man. This is the believer's duty according to the command of Christ.

"And the second is like unto it,
Thou shalt love thy neighbour as
thyself."
—Matthew 22:39

Love dictates sensitivity and tactfulness, without it, the evidence of love is diminished. The words that flow from our mouths are to be weighty sayings that bring pleasure, delight, and joy to the hearer.

Furthermore, it should enable the hearer to thrive and benefit. If they are crushed by, tactless words how will they thrive when fed with spiritual poison?

"A merry heart doeth good like a
medicine: but a broken spirit
drieth the bones."
—Proverbs 17:22

The Greek meaning of the word grace is loving-kindness, affection, and good will. It is to have holy influence upon souls and to turn others to Christ. Jesus will judge all our words by this standard.

"But I say unto you, That every
idle word that men shall speak,
they shall give account thereof in
the day of judgment."
—Matthew 12:36

*"So then every one of us shall
give account of himself to God."*
—Romans 12:12

Our words are to be a gift to the hearer,
which they choose to either accept, reject,
or place it on a shelf for a later time.
When we allow God to help us in our
speaking process our words will be
properly prepared (seasoned with salt).
Only then will they be able to fulfill their
divine purpose of uplifting, planting,
carrying, bearing, feeding, or correcting
the hearer. If the Spirit of God does not
prepare our words, then they are evil for
they spring forth from the flesh, and not
from the Spirit of God.

*"Then the LORD put forth his
hand, and touched my mouth.
And the LORD said unto me,
Behold, I have put my words in
thy mouth."*
—Jeremiah 1:9

*"I am the LORD thy God, which
brought thee out of the land of
Egypt: open thy mouth wide, and
I will fill it."*
—Psalms 81:10

God has delivered us from the land of
captivity. He desires to fill our mouths
with His Words. If we open our mouths in

faith, He will fill them with words that will please and glorify Him.

> *"How sweet are thy words unto*
> *my taste! yea, sweeter than*
> *honey to my mouth!"*
> —Psalms 119:103

> *"And he said unto me, Son of*
> *man, cause thy belly to eat, and*
> *fill thy bowels with this roll that I*
> *give thee. Then did I eat it; and it*
> *was in my mouth as honey for*
> *sweetness."*
> —Ezekiel 3:3

> *"Pleasant words are as an*
> *honeycomb, sweet to the soul,*
> *and health to the bones."*
> —Proverbs 16:24

Gracious words prepared by the Spirit of God will bless the soul, body, and life of the hearer. It is time for our mouths to be a *continual* blessing and spring of life on the earth.

DAY 7

Brethren, we are called to love our neighbors as ourselves. Therefore, before we speak we should take time to consider our words and our attitudes. The tactless tongue has wounded many in the body of Christ.

Yet if we take the time to ask ourselves if we were addressing Jesus would we still speak what is on our mind? Or will our words or attitude ensure that we will meet him upon his return? Would we refine our words or adjust our attitude if we stopped for a moment to reflect realizing that Christ is present when we speak?

Christ dwells within us. He is present in every conversation! Our brothers and sisters in Christ have the same spirit of Christ in them. When we treat them tactlessly, we are doing it unto him, and Holy Spirit is a witness.

> *"And the King shall answer and say unto them, Verily I say unto you, Inasmuch as ye have done it unto one of the least of these my brethren, ye have done it unto me."*
> —Matthew 25:40

And he said, Who art thou, Lord?
And the Lord said, I am Jesus
whom thou persecutest: it is hard
for thee to kick against the
pricks."

—Acts 9:5

Prayer

My Father, who art in heaven hear my prayer, oh Lord. Help me to be quick to listen and slow to speak. Help my spirit to be patient and not hasty. Remove folly from me and fill me with wisdom and prudence. Be glorified in my speaking, I ask in Jesus name, amen.

"Wherefore, my beloved
brethren, let every man be swift
to hear, slow to speak, slow to
wrath:"

—James 1:19

He that is slow to wrath is of
great understanding: but he that
is hasty of spirit exalteth folly."

—Proverbs 14:29

Activity

This week take a personal inventory of the conversations you have. If possible, use a little black book to record incidences where you have spoken tactless words. If you cannot remember or are not sure if the words you spoke were tactless ask Holy Spirit. He will lead you to *all* truth (John 16:13).

As we go forward on our journey with God, His Spirit will lead, guide, and correct us. God wants spiritual fruit to manifest in our lives, so we are assured that Jesus will help us if we ask believing (John 14:13 and Galatians 5:22).

Disease of the

REPROACHFUL TONGUE

"He that backbiteth not with his tongue, nor doeth evil to his neighbour, nor taketh up a reproach against his neighbor."
—Psalms 15:3

The reproachful tongue rests upon the shame or disgrace of another. It taunts, openly resists, and refuses to obey the command of God concerning the treatment of a neighbor.

This type of tongue is willing to jeopardize the harvest of God by finding fault with another, plucking off any spiritual fruit that may have started to sprout in the Lord by covering the person in humiliation and dishonor.

"Who hate the good, and love the evil; who pluck off their skin from off them, and their flesh from off their bones;"
—Micah 3:2

"Thus saith the LORD against all mine evil neighbours, that touch the inheritance which I have caused my people Israel to inherit; Behold, I will pluck them out of their land, and pluck out the house of Judah from among them."
—Jeremiah 12:14

Our mission by God is to build one another up from the foundation.

"Wherefore comfort yourselves together, and edify one another, even as also ye do."
—1 Thessalonians 5:11

We are to be master builders after the likeness of Christ (Matthew 16:18).

"According to the grace of God which is given unto me, as a wise masterbuilder, I have laid the foundation, and another buildeth thereon. But let every man take heed how he buildeth thereupon."
—1 Corinthians 3:10

Each of us is responsible for how and what we build (1 Corinthians 3:11-23). Let us seek to build one another (up) in love, thus making manifest the character and nature of God to all around us.

DAY 8

There are those among us who take pleasure in the shame or down fall of others. They *despise hearing good news* but salivate when they get a whiff of scandal.

They are not interested in helping to build, exhort, or encourage others but rather to tear at their flesh like a wolf. Christ did not come to create wolves; he came to raise sheep who are willing to lay down their lives for others.

All that is good, decent, and respectable about us rests in Jesus. We have no cause to allow our tongues to be reproachful toward anyone. All of us are sinners *saved by grace* and without the gift of God's *grace;* none of us would have a hope of sharing in the glory of Christ.

Prayer

Purify my tongue oh Lord. Cleanse it with hyssop (Psalms 51:7). I repent for covering others with shame and disgrace. I've used my mouth as a weapon. Help me to be a spring of life for all those who hear the words of my mouth. Cause my words to be pleasing to Your ears (Psalms 19:14). Let them water, fertilize, and nourish all around me, I pray in Jesus name, amen.

Activity

Refuse to rehash past grievances or recount past failures (of others or your own). Refuse to cover yourself or your neighbor in shame and dishonor.

Instead, seek the beauty in your experiences. The lessons learned or benefits acquired. If you cannot identify any, ask God to reveal them to you, both natural and spiritual.

"He hath made every thing beautiful in his time: also he hath set the world in their heart, so that no man can find out the work that God maketh from the beginning to the end."
Ecclesiastes 3:11

God has made everything beautiful in its own time. As He removes our shame, He reveals the beauty of understanding, knowledge, and wisdom.

> *"Fear not; for thou shalt not be ashamed: neither be thou confounded; for thou shalt not be put to shame: for thou shalt forget the shame of thy youth, and shalt not remember the reproach of thy widowhood any more."*
> —Isaiah 54:4

> *"Turn away my reproach which I fear: for thy judgments are good."*
> —Psalms 119:39

The ways of God are good, His counsel infallible, and His wisdom beyond measure.

Disease of the

KNOW-IT-ALL TONGUE

*And if any man think that he
knoweth any thing, he knoweth
nothing yet as he ought to know."*
—1 Corinthians 8:2

In 1 Corinthians 8:2 Paul makes a remarkable statement according to the Greek understanding of the verse. In plain terms Paul asserts, he would not talk about any man in particular, but a man in general who has determined for himself that he rightly discerns anything about a person or a thing, this man knows nothing to the degree he ought to know the person or thing!

Paul concedes that the man could have conducted interviews, visited with the individual, researched the thing, and obtained knowledge. He could have observed with his eyes, perceived with his senses, or experienced it personally. Yet Paul declares the man still knows **nothing**, *as he ought to know it.*

This know-it-all man does not discern what is right and proper, he does not understand the nature of the case or the necessity brought on by the circumstances. He does not comprehend what is at the root of the person's actions or what caused the situation. He is not acquainted with the reasons, nor has he been brought into correct knowledge of *all* the facts.

> *"Be not wise in thine own eyes: fear the LORD, and depart from evil."*
> —Proverbs 3:7

If we know-it-all then *what* can God teach us? What can we learn from God? The know-it-all tongue hinders us from obtaining spiritual discernment. It blocks us from being taught in every situation by the Lord. It will take us the way of evil.

The choice is ours. Will we depart from evil? Will we confess and repent to God? Will we admit that we do not know-it-all? If so, it will restore our health.

> *"It shall be health to thy navel, and marrow to thy bones."*
> —Proverbs 3:8

If not it will destroy us from the inside out, because *we will not know as we ought to know!*

DAY 9

It is hard to teach a know-it-all anything, because they turn off their mind to learning and stuff their ears with cotton so they cannot hear. Those who purport themselves as possessing knowledge (worldly) have none.

Those who recognize that they are in need of knowledge (God) possess it all. The Bible says that the fear of the Lord is the beginning of wisdom. If a person possesses a high IQ and does not have an intimate knowledge of God, he is foolish.

The simple truth is that in order to increase in knowledge one has to be willing to humble oneself to learn. A know-it-all will refuse to do so. Therefore, he will have to be humbled by the Lord. Pharaoh was humbled by God, as was Nebuchadnezzar.

As a child of God, opt to humble yourself rather than provoking God to have to humble you.

Prayer

Lord, I confess my sin before you. I have spoken with a know-it-all tongue. I ask for Your forgiveness. Father, I desire to know, as I ought to know, with spiritual discernment. Help me not to be wise in my own eyes, and not to walk in the way of evil. Cause health to come to my navel and marrow to my bones (Proverbs 3:7-8). I pray, amen.

Activity

Today refuse to be a know-it-all. Be a student willing to learn from everyone. Allow your friends, teachers, boss, coworkers, children or family to share what they know with you. Ask God to be your filter, let Him identify what is good and beneficial for you. Hold on to what is good in word, lesson, report, or prophesy (1 Thessalonians 5:21).

"Finally, brethren, whatsoever things are true, whatsoever things are honest, whatsoever things are just, whatsoever things are pure, whatsoever things are lovely, whatsoever things are of good report; if there be any virtue, and if there be any praise, think on these things."
—Philippians 4:8

Disease of the

OFFENSIVE TONGUE

"For in many things we offend all. If any man offend not in word, the same is a perfect man, and able also to bridle the whole body."
—James 3:2

O ne may believe that an offensive tongue is one that causes someone to get angry, to become upset or to hurt deeply and while that may be true in our modern understanding of the word **offend** it is not what God considers offensive.

An offensive tongue according to the Greek meaning is one that causes someone to descend from an erect position to a prostrate one. It is to cause another to fall or stumble by the words one speaks. It is to cause another to become unfruitful or to die (fall under judgement or condemnation) by the words spoken.

If our words cause someone to enter into a winter, where they are unfruitful, become cold, or they appear to be dead spiritually then we have offended with our tongue.

Our words are to be life giving, they are to nourish and provide nutrients to all those who hear them. Our words are to create the optimal conditions for growth and for the sustenance of life. Wherein our words fail to be a fountain of life, then they are contrary to the purpose and plan of God, therefore they are **offensive**.

An offensive tongue is one that is under the control of the enemy attacking those who the Lord desires to bring into relationship with himself or those he desires to encourage in the ways of life.

An offensive tongue assaults, charges, or to wars against the way things are to be ordered according to the standard of God.

What does James mean? When he says, *"For in many things we offend all."* In numerous or countless things, we (both you and I) have caused others to fall. Our words were like a gulf or pit, which has caused others to fall down into the darkness, to stumble, or to err. We have caused others to move from a sure and steady foundation to tumbling downward in the air as a bird descending from the sky when it is about to perch or land on a tree branch.

At some point in our lives, we *all* have been guilty of this offense. If we do not offend with our tongues then we would be perfect and therefore able to control our bodies.

The remedy for an offensive tongue is a **bridle**. Our *bridle* is powerful and never fails when it is utilized. The only thing that can control the mouth of man is the power of God though the work of Christ Jesus.

Jesus was the only man who by his words never caused an offense to God, for his words were and are life and light unto all those who hear and receive them.

DAY 10

Honor the Lord with the fruit of your lips. Let your words be sweet and tasty unto him.

"By him therefore let us offer the sacrifice of praise to God continually, that is, the fruit of our lips giving thanks to his name."
—Hebrews 13:15

Train yourself in the ways of *life*. Speak words of life. Build rather than destroy, encourage rather than insult, help others to grow stronger and more firm in the ways of God, rather than discouraged and condemned.

God has given us an important mission that is to be *life givers*. We extend oxygen to those who are in danger of dying. We help resuscitate those who have succumb to the pressures and challenges of life. We are light to those engulfed in darkness, and we are the hope for those who are in need.

When we fail to carry out our mission, we are an offense to God because we are not acting or operating like him but rather like the enemy.

When God looks at us, he wants to see Christ. When our fragrance reaches his nostrils, it is to be a sweet smelling fragrance and not a foul odor. When Satan goes before the Lord to accuse us, he should have *nothing* to say.

May God have cause to boast on us as he did Job. May he have reason to honor us among men and in the presence of angels!

Prayer

Father, forgive me of my sins of offense. I have spoken words, which have dishonored you. I have used my mouth as a weapon against others and at times even myself. Blot out my offenses; cast them into the sea of forgetfulness.

Lord, help me that from this day my mouth will be a spring of life and encouragement to all who hear the words I speak. Season my words with love but let them ever speak the truth. Help me to be kind and patient with others and with myself, as you are loving, kind, and patient with me.

May all that I do bring glory to your name, I pray, amen.

Activity

Today you may be tested and it is up to you to rely on God for strength. You have prayed and he has heard you! Stand firm in faith, believing, that he will do as he has promised. Victory is yours . . . in Jesus name. If things get too trying, cry out for increased strength. Remember if you resist the enemy, he *will flee* from you.

Disease of the

EXCESSIVE TALKING TONGUE

"In the multitude of words there wanteth not sin: but he that refraineth his lips [is] wise"
—Proverbs 10:19

Have you ever been around an individual who talks constantly? A person whose mouth goes faster than humming bird's wings? Have you found it a challenge to get a word in edgewise? It is a wonder that he or she is able to breathe!

Excessive talking is not considered abnormal today because so many people do it! According to Proverbs, 10:19 sin is intertwined with a multitude of words. Why does the Bible say this? Could it be that when we speak without taking time to think we are more apt to say something that is not true? Could this be viewed as a lie in God's book? Perhaps.

You may be wondering, what's so wrong about excessive speaking?

Ecclesiastes 5:3 tells us that a fool's voice is known by a multitude of words. Thus, an excessive talker is identified as a *fool* according to the word of the Lord not because of what he says but by how much he says. Very few people want to be thought of or identified as a fool; in fact, most people want to be seen as wise and full of knowledge. The bottom line is that excessive talking is not the way to make a wise impression.

The Bible tells us that a person who can control (hold) his tongue is wise (Ecclesiastes 5:3). Thus if we want to be considered wise we should follow the advice of Jesus in Matthew 5:37,

> *"But let your communication be,*
> *Yea, yea; Nay, nay: for*
> *whatsoever is more than these*
> *cometh of evil."*

By following Jesus' advice we are practicing to restrain the tongue which is wise (Proverbs 10:19).

As believers in Christ Jesus we should use few words to say what needs to be said and then lock up our tongues (place them under subjection). By doing this we force ourselves to think before we speak. In order to speak few words we have to know exactly what we want to communicate and by the grace of God, we will know the best and clearest way to do so before we utter a word.

James tells us that we should be quick to listen, slow to speak and slow to get angry (James 1:19). As we listen, we are to think about what we are hearing. By not rushing to get angry, we can focus on the real issue and then address the issue after we have carefully thought it through.

Have you been diagnosed with the excessive talking disease? Are you ready to be healed from it? All you need to do is make a decision to apply the Word of the Lord to your life. Decide to follow the counsel of Jesus and let your "Yea" be "Yea" and your "Nay" be "Nay."

Be determined that you will apply the
advice of James and be quick to listen and
slow to speak. By doing so, you are
getting off the path of the fool and
entering the road of the wise.

DAY 11

There are those among us who need to set a watch over their mouths in order to be preserved blameless before God.

In order to establish a watch, we must admit that we need help. God is willing and able to assist us in this matter, but we have to be willing to seek his help.

> *"And the very God of peace sanctify you wholly; and I pray God your whole spirit and soul and body be preserved blameless unto the coming of our Lord Jesus Christ."*
> —1 Thessalonians 5:23

Each one of us has been guilty of offending with our tongues. Each one of us has unclean lips. Even though they are unclean, they do not have to remain so! God is able to clean it with coals of fire (Isaiah 6:6).

*"Then said I, Woe is me! for I am
undone; because I am a man of
unclean lips, and I dwell in the
midst of a people of unclean lips:
for mine eyes have seen the King,
the LORD of hosts."*

—Isaiah 6:5

All we need do is to ask believing.

Prayer

Father, I thank you for your word, which is life and light unto me. I bless you because you have called me to be wise in you. Lord help me that I will forever leave the ways of the foolish.

Father, if I have ensnared people with my words forgive me. If my words have opened the way for sin to take up residence within my being, I repent. Cleanse me from all unrighteousness.

Enable me to manage my words in righteousness and sound judgment. Help me to be a beacon of light to those around me. Let my words be a spring of life and not a dead sea. These mercies I ask in Jesus name, amen.

Activity

Record a few of your interactions today. Later play them back and note the times when you used too many words and said something, which was not true, where you gossiped, or where your words may have hurt someone.

After you have reviewed the recording, ask God how you can make it right with him, with yourself, and with others.

By doing this, you are exposing the excessive talking tongue to the light of God. Eventually it will have nowhere to hide and it will leave, because there will be no place for it.

DAY 12

Disease of the

LYING TONGUE

*"Lying lips are abomination to
the LORD: but they that deal
truly are his delight"*
—Proverbs 12:22

Lying, what does it mean to lie? According to the Hebrew meaning, the word *lying* is deception, fraud, trickery, cheating, speaking with a false tongue, dealing falsely, and disappointment. It is also when one is false to one's faith or when one breaks a covenant.

White lies or black lies...which one does God prefer?

A lie is a lie! —And a lie is sin for it originates with the father of lies—Satan— according to the word of God (John 8:44). Proverbs 12:22, tells us that lying lips are an abomination to the Lord.

This means that lying lips disgust him. They cause abhorrence and it doesn't matter the reason for the lie—whether it is to protect someone, or to keep from getting into trouble, to be able to get your own way, or to avoid hurting someone's feelings, etc. —they are all considered a lie.

So what can we do when a lie seems easier and less complicated than the truth? Or when the truth will hurt? We can make a decision to tell the truth no matter what. For truth delights the Lord.

> *"Hear; for I will speak of excellent things; and the opening of my lips shall be right things. For my mouth shall speak truth; and wickedness is an abomination to my lips. All the words of my mouth are in righteousness; there is nothing forward or perverse in them"*
> —Proverbs 8:6-8.

If you make the decision for truth, it will be easier to speak the truth at all times even when the truth can or will hurt the hearer.

Proverbs 27:6 says,

> *"Faithful are the wounds of a friend; but the kisses of an enemy are deceitful."*

According to The American Heritage College Dictionary, the word *faithful* means consistent with truth. Therefore this verse is stating that consistent with truth are the wounds of a friend. If you truly love or care for a person you will honor him or her by speaking the truth. If you find it easier to lie, you are not demonstrating love, honor, or sincere friendship.

God consistently honors us by speaking truth to us. It is this truth that sanctifies and purifies us (John 17:17, Psalms 119:160). Jesus is truth (John 14:6). Holy Spirit is the Spirit of Truth (John 14:16-17).

God is looking for those who will worship Him in spirit and in truth (John 4:23). (How we live and move in his presence, which is more than just being at church).

Part of our armor as believers is the belt of truth (Ephesians 16:14). If we want to walk with God, it must be with truth as our constant companion!

When we do this our lives will be a fragrance of worship before the Lord that will honor him and bring him delight.

The Word of God is clear . . . lying lips are an abomination to God; they are disgusting, detestable, and loathsome to him. Therefore, we know that God will not sanction or approve a lie, though he is always willing to forgive us if we confess our sins before him, he will never condone lying.

DAY 12

Often little children when confronted by a parent or an adult about something they did will quickly devise a lie. Fear has gripped their little hearts and they believe that if the truth were known it would be worse than speaking a lie.

Unfortunately, many adults have failed to grow up, and still operate as little children when confronted by others. God knows the truth and since he knows it what does it matter if man also is made aware of the truth?

There is no man on earth who has a heaven or hell to put us in nor does he determine your final destiny. Lying words will ultimately pave our way to hell unless we turn from it.

It is the fear of the Lord not the fear of man, which is the beginning of wisdom. Let us therefore in wisdom bridle the lying tongue by the power of the spirit of truth.

Prayer

Father, in the name of Jesus, help me to walk in truth. Renew my mind and fashion my words after truth. Forgive me wherein I have lied knowingly or unknowingly. It is my desire to walk intentionally in the way of truth.

Lord distinguish me from others who love lies, and enjoy creating lies. Set me a part. Establish a wall of division between them and me. Cause my light to shine brightly for Jesus in all that I do and in each word that I speak, in Jesus name, amen.

Activity

Today observe others as they speak with you. Are they lovers of truth? Or do they love lies and crafting them? If they love lies, ask God for wisdom so that you can address the situation in love according to his will.

Does he want you to speak with them? If so, he will fill your mouth with the right words and your heart with the right attitude.

Does he want you to terminate the fellowship? Then he will give you an unction in your spirit and will guide you in the proper way to terminate the relationship.

Or does he want you to extend a helping hand to gently *expose* them to the light of Jesus, the truth of God so that their soul can be won to Jesus?

Whatever direction God desires to lead you in, you have to decide if you are willing to follow him all the way.

Before you can lead others into truth you must be established in it, therefore you cannot be a lover of lies!

DAY 13

Disease of the

FLATTERING TONGUE

"A man that flattereth his neighbour spreadeth a net for his feet"
—Proverbs 29:5

In this age of moral decline, it is hard to find godly people who speak truth consistently. Because of this, many people engage in speaking lies to their neighbor uttering words of flattery with their lips, which are used to deceive (Psalms 12:1-3).

What is flattery really? It is when complements are given excessively, often, and in most cases insincerely. They are words spoken with the intent to deceive, manipulate, or to win favor with an individual or group. You may be thinking, "What is wrong with complementing someone?"

Flattery is not a complement. When you complement someone, you are giving a person sincere or honest praise for an achievement. Complements are based in truth, while flattery is based in a lie, which is intended to mislead or take advantage of an individual.

God considers flattery a serious offense. In Psalms 12:3, David tells us what the Lord will do to those with flattering lips,

> *"The LORD shall cut off all flattering lips, [and] the tongue that speaketh proud things:...."*

Why would God cut off those who engage in this pastime? Because,

> *"A lying tongue hateth [those that are] afflicted by it; and a flattering mouth worketh ruin"*
> —Proverbs 26:28.

A flatterer does not reflect the character of Christ, which is one of love, truth, honesty, and integrity. The fruit of flattery comes from a tree of hate, lying, and deceit. The word tells us that by our fruit we shall be known (Matthew 7:16-20).

If flattery is our fruit, from which tree do we come? However, if truth is our fruit then it is clear to whom we belong. What is your fruit?

DAY13

Have you ever told someone that you loved her hair style or dress when secretly you criticized it? Or have you commended someone on a job well done when in your mind you had a list of things that he did wrong, and your true thought and feeling was that he totally messed it up?

If you have then you were guilty of a flattering tongue. There is a multitude of reasons, why you chose to speak words of untruth, but the bottom-line is that you were not complementing the person with lips of sincerity or truth!

Your words mislead and misrepresented your true feeling and intentions. Joshua was tricked into a covenant with the Gibeonites according to Joshua 9.

They lavished fine words on Joshua about his God and his great exploits. Although the words were true their hearts were deceptive, and their objective was to secure a covenantal relationship with the children of Israel.

What is your objective when you butter others up with flattering words? If what you say is not pure and true in actuality and robed in sincerity from the heart than it ought not to be said.

Prayer

Father, I repent for using a flattering tongue. For speaking words which were not true and sincere. Fill my heart with genuine love for others. Cause my heart to be a wellspring of truth.

Let my words bring glory and honor to you. Let them not be a snare to others as they travel into glory, in the name of Jesus.

Activity

Today take some time to review your interactions with others over the last few days or weeks. Have you constantly spoken the truth? Were there times when you manipulated or deceived others? Did your words reflect the character of Christ?

If not then ask Holy Spirit to guide you into what you ought to do. Holy Spirit will never lead you into sin but will steer your course into righteousness and right standing with God.

Disease of the

GOSSIPING TONGUE

"The words of a talebearer [are]
as wounds, and they go down
into the innermost parts of the
belly"
—Proverbs 18:8

M any believers are in the advance stages of the disease of gossip. Other sins are easier to identify and speak boldly against, but there is something about gossip that causes many to stop short of calling it a sin much less a disease of the tongue. Gossip is a disease which is more deadly than cancer for it can place us under the condemnation of God on the Day of Judgment (Matthew 12:37).

What is gossip? *Gossip* is slander—idle, exaggerated, untrue, malicious talk, even when we think we are being entertaining, we can be gossiping, if we are talking about real people and their situations.

In Leviticus 19:16, the Bible tells us not to spread slander. Therefore, it is wrong to engage in this pastime for it betrays a confidence (Proverbs 20:19). *Gossip* is a sin whether we are spreading news or receiving news, for the Word of God tells us to avoid people who talk too much (gossip).

The cancerous cells of gossip are detrimental to healthy relationships. They wage war within relationships stirring up negativity, opposing kingdom living, and can even result in spiritual murder.

Gossip morsels go down into our innermost parts and have the tendency to taint, corrupt, or poison our view of others and they can destroy pleasant, sweet, or peaceful affiliations with our brethren.

Furthermore, gossip can cause us to express disappointment, disapproval, or unleash criticism against another.

Gossip blocks us from establishing and maintaining loving and harmonious connections with fellow believers and with God (Psalms 15:1-3). If you have been guilty of gossiping against others or have been allowing others to speak words of gossip in your ears, it is not too late to turn from this sinful pastime.

If you desire to abide in the tent of the Lord... if you want to be justified (vindicated, and declared righteous) on that great Day...if you truly want to have the character of Christ alive in you take this step toward your eternal destiny— eliminate gossip!

> *"And every man that hath this hope in him purifieth himself, even as he is pure."*
>
> —1 John 3:3

It is time to purify yourself.

DAY 14

Why do we gossip? Why do so many find it so sweet to do so? Does it somehow make us feel that we are better than another? Does it feed our ego?

No matter the reason, gossiping is a sin and therefore it is wrong for us to engage in it. We are called to build one another up. How does gossip enable us to achieve that directive?

By spreading news about another's situation, we are sowing webs, which will ensnare and complicate the person's life unnecessarily. Christ admonishes us to love our neighbor as we love our selves. How many of us want to be the subject of gossip? Or to have our business bouncing around on the street like a dirty rag?

If we would not like it for ourselves, we should not do it to others.

Prayer

Purify me, oh Lord. Cleanse me from unrighteousness. My mouth has committed murder against your people, against my family, and even against my friends.

I have allowed my words to pour out like a raging flood and I ask you to forgive me.

Father, touch my lips with your coals of fire. Cause my mouth to become a spring of life and hope, building up and not tearing down, in the name of Jesus.

Father, wherein others have been injured I pray that you will release healing unto them. Wherein their reputation has been soiled, I ask that you restore unto them their good name, in Jesus name I pray, amen.

Activity

Today write down a list of those you have sinned against through gossip. Are they still alive?

Then ask God to help you humble yourself before them and go confess your sin to them. When you remember to seal the relationship in prayer always asking God to establish love, forgiveness, and peace in the both your hearts.

If they are no longer alive or you do not know where or how to find them, ask God to remove any guilt, shame, or condemnation from you. Pray in his peace, joy, and love so you can move forward in the abundant grace of the Lord.

Disease of the

UNBRIDLED TONGUE

"But the tongue can no man tame; it is an unruly evil, full of deadly poison."
—James 3:8

Many believe they can do all things if they put their mind to it. They can accomplish great feats, achieve wondrous goals, or change the course of history through sheer will (or self) power. Historical records attest to the fact that several men have achieved this honor (men of renowned Genesis 6:4) over the centuries, yet James tells us that no man has been able to tame the smallest member of the human body!

Man for all his trying cannot tame the tongue by virtue of man's own ability or resources, not by favorable circumstances, not by strength or power, nor by permission of custom or law. *Nothing* that man has access to in the natural realm can aid or enable him to *bridle* (curb, restrain, or tame) his tongue.

The *unbridled tongue* has a bad nature; it operates in a way that ought not to be, for it is based in wrong thoughts and feelings. It is injurious, destructive, wicked, and it stirs up trouble. It is full of evil.

It is a bringer of death, misery, and causes separation (spiritually, naturally or through violence) of the body and soul. It is as poisonous as rust is to metal, leading to a life of wretchedness in hell. Unless . . .

James tells us that the tongue is unruly, meaning it cannot be restrained except by the Alpha, the one who is the beginning and the end. He alone possesses the resources necessary for man to bridle his fiery and evil tongue.

If you have an infirmity of the tongue, there is a special word of encouragement for you.

"And he said unto me, My grace is sufficient for thee: for my strength is made perfect in weakness. Most gladly therefore will I rather glory in my infirmities, that the power of Christ may rest upon me."
—2 Corinthians 12:9

Paul notes that if boasting is needed, boast about what pertains to weakness. Christ came to help the weak since the strong can fend for themselves.

> *"If I must needs glory, I will glory of the things which concern mine infirmities.*
> —2 Corinthians 11:30

> *"I can do all things through Christ which strengtheneth me."*
> —Philippians 4:13

If we allow Christ to strengthen us then we will not sin with our tongues, we will keep our mouths with bridles, and we will be deemed a perfect man capable of curbing our whole body.

> *"[[To the chief Musician, even to Jeduthun, A Psalm of David.]] I said, I will take heed to my ways, that I sin not with my tongue: I will keep my mouth with a bridle, while the wicked is before me."*
> —Psalms 39:1

> *"For in many things we offend all. If any man offend not in word, the same is a perfect man, and able also to bridle the whole body."*
> —James 3:2

DAY 15

The wicked are observant. They are studying you. They are looking for a crack in your armor. They want to accuse you, to call you a hypocrite, a liar, a false disciple of Christ.

Do not give them cause to ridicule you. You are Jesus' representative in the earth. You are to reflect his nature as he reflected God's own.

When you allow an unbridled tongue to soil your garments or poison your witness, it reflects negatively on Jesus. This is what happened when David sinned with Bathsheba. David was God's man, the one who was to do the will of God.

> "And when he had removed him, he raised up unto them David to be their king; to whom also he gave testimony, and said, I have found David the son of Jesse, a man after mine own heart, which shall fulfil all my will."

—Acts 13:22

David was punished because his actions were sinful. If his sin were left unpunished, it would have reflected negatively on God thus conveying the wrong message about God and his kingdom.

God's standard is nonnegotiable! If we choose to do our own thing, we will not get away scot-free.

Prayer

Father, I thank you for your grace, which is sufficient to meet any challenge and to deal with every situation.

The Spirit of grace is able to tame my *unbridled* tongue. Your grace can strengthen me. Your grace can establish me. Father, set me firmly in the presence of your grace. Cause your grace to follow me, to guide me, and to keep me.

Father, bless the words of my mouth. Let them be filled with truth, life, hope, forgiveness, and joy. When I speak, speak through me. Hide me behind the cross of Jesus and cover me under his blood.

Let me not be an offense in the land. Let me not cause others to stumble and fall. Keep my hands clean from the blood of the innocent. May I be an encouragement, a comfort, and a support to your people, this I pray in the name of Jesus, amen.

Activity

Today see God, allow him to identify areas in which your tongue still needs to be bridled. You are able to do all things through Jesus Christ who strengthens you!

CONCLUSION

As believers, we are charged with a solemn task. God will not do it for us, though He will strongly support us if we choose to do it (2 Chronicles 16:9). We have to choose to live in the light. Our existence as sons of God demands that we love light, desire to be near the light, and that we are bearers of light (John 1:5, Acts 17:11, and 1 John 1:5).

If we hate light, prefer darkness, dabble in secret sins, or occasionally stroll in the shadows then we are breaking our covenant vows with God.

God has made a way for us to follow His example; it is not an impossible task for Christ did it by the power of God. Our Father has even stacked the deck in our favor by sending Holy Spirit to reside with us on the earth. Even more importantly, the entire Godhead exists and lives in us if we choose to allow them to help us clean house.

"Jesus answered and said unto him, If a man love me, he will keep my words: and my Father will love him, and we will come unto him, and make our abode with him."

—John 14:23

"Or else how can one enter into a strong man's house, and spoil his goods, except he first bind the strong man? and then he will spoil his house."

—Matthew 12:29

"He that committeth sin is of the devil; for the devil sinneth from the beginning. For this purpose the Son of God was manifested, that he might destroy the works of the devil."

—1 John 3:8

Christ alone is the true strongman. He came to destroy the works of the devil and He did, for Satan was condemned (John 12:30-31 and John 16:10-11).

When we allow Christ to be Lord of our lives He will continue to manifest His power by breaking, destroying, shaking, burning, eliminating and delivering us from the works of the devil and from the darkness that dwells within (Mark 7:15, 20) and around us (Romans 7:21).

As we believe and operate by the authority Christ we too will become strongmen able to destroy the works of the devil (Luke 10:19) and help others to do the same to the glory of God.

May God continue to bless you as you walk deeper into the light of his presence!

www.ingramcontent.com/pod-product-compliance
Lightning Source LLC
Chambersburg PA
CBHW031628040426
42452CB00007B/729